EAT

the foods available and enjoyed
by the ancient Greeks and Romans

DRINK

Water and wine and the traditions
which grew up around them

AND
BE MERRY

how people enjoyed themselves
and the changing fashions
of entertainment and manners
in Greek and Roman Times

AUDREY BRIERS

ASHMOLEAN MUSEUM · OXFORD

Illustrations

The drawings of cooking utensils, ovens and bee-hives were made by the author from originals in Greek Museums. The herbs, most of which are native to the Aegean and Mediterranean, were also drawn by the author. The photographs are all from the Ashmolean Museum's collections – from decorated Greek vases (drinking cups and jugs) of the fifth and sixth centuries B.C., and from coins of Athens, Crete, Rhodes and other Aegean islands including Melos and Thasos and from Cyrene, on the North African coast.

The pottery jugs and cups are made from clay, unless otherwise mentioned, and most are black and terracotta in colour. The herbs can all be obtained today except for silphium, although different varieties are often in cultivation now. For example, the wild parsley in the drawing has been developed to make the curled variety used today.

The list of books at the end will give more information on all these subjects and these books are available from Public Libraries if requested. The amusing and chatty volumes by Athenaeus will give an idea of the general background. If you would like Roman recipes, the translation of Apicius will provide excellent examples.

Other titles by Audrey Briers published by the Ashmolean Museum:
TRUE STORIES ABOUT MONEY
TRUE STORIES OF COINS AND KINGS
TRUE STORIES ABOUT ROMAN COINS
TRUE STORIES ABOUT GREEK COINS

Drawings by Audrey Briers
Designed by Andrew Ivett
Typeset in Zapf International and Zapf Chancery by
Meridian Phototypesetting Ltd, Pangbourne
Printed and bound in Great Britain by
Cheney and Sons Limited, Banbury, 1990

Time and Place

THE TIME is 2000 B.C. and the place is Greece. From about this point we begin to find clues to the development of civil life in Europe. Other civilizations had existed before 2000 B.C. but the Greeks created an environment of their own. The benefits which followed were later to continue in Rome and down to our own times.

So, for our purposes, 'early Greek' will mean before about 1000 B.C. and 'Greek' will mean the years until the Romans became more important and numerous at the start of the Roman Empire. 'Late Roman' will mean the 3rd-4th centuries A.D. – you will see the difference in eating habits and developing life-styles as time passes.

The entire population of the Greek world in 2000 B.C. was less than one million instead of about 10 million in modern Greece today and people lived in communities isolated from each other. Their world was small, local, fringed with other tribes who might hunt in the dense forests inhabited by deer, bears, wolves and birds. The secret dark groves and caves were impressive and alarming to people armed only with stone or bronze weapons, so the ancient Gods and Goddesses were often worshipped there.

The largest towns would be very small by modern standards, with a head man or woman – a King or Queen – to rule over them. Gradually these towns became cities – still small, but places where people could trade their surplus food and goods. Many of these cities became famous for one particular product and all would have had a market-place.

This background was old by the time this book begins. Good times were there, but we hear only faint memories of them – perhaps no less accurate for that – because all we have to go on are the stories handed down by word of mouth, the repeated songs of early poets, and finally, the written word from about 500 B.C. onwards.

The eating, drinking, and the occasional orgy, were often done with one eye on the Gods. If a God liked dancing, well, let's make the most of it and have a party! The sacrifice of meat to a God was still a sacrifice even if there was a feast afterwards with the remainder.

No God seemed to think the worse of anyone for enjoying themselves after the holy rites had been given their proper place. So eat, drink and be merry for, at the moment, all is well!

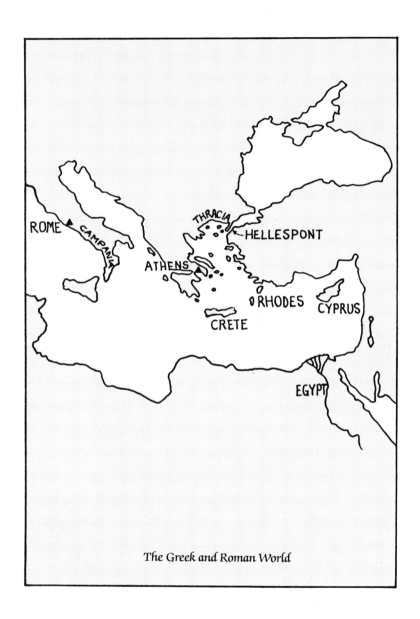

The Greek and Roman World

EAT

THE SHARP AND SPICY TANG of Greek and Roman cookery became more complicated and noticeable as time went on. Although more wooded than today, the landscape itself, mostly high, dry and mountainous, produced herbs and plants which are still the very stuff of sauces and savoury dishes. The enticing smell of a South European kitchen must have been much the same for the last three thousand years. But there was food to eat long before that.

In the days of the hunter, meat and plants were brought back to the home hearth to be eaten in a group gathered round the fire. It was a social occasion, a time of meeting and recognition, for exchange of talk about the day's excitements. The early Greek hunters killed wild game in the forests – such as deer and wild pig – and wild birds came from the marshlands and river banks. These were roasted over an open fire, someone turning the spit on which the meat was held, and when it was cooked, taking off pieces with knives and fingers. All the food was equally divided among the group with great care, including barley cakes and wine. Guests and honoured people were offered the tastiest portions as a sign of respect. Eating was done sitting upright, in an orderly formal way. In later centuries Greeks who considered themselves to be modern, smiled at the notion of roasting meat by this method as old-fashioned, and took their meals reclining on couches, as the Romans also did by then.

By 500 B.C., the population of the Greek homelands had doubled and the Greek appetite for food had altered and broadened. All sorts of changes had taken place, particularly in the growing and improvement of vegetables and fruit. Meat became a less important part of the diet and a whole variety of vegetables, salads, fruit, nuts, dried fruit and sweet cakes became available.

With such a climate and rich soil almost anything will grow if water can be found at the right time. The early rains were of first importance, but when they ended, irrigation and the use of storage cisterns supplemented the natural springs and fountains. Crops of wheat and barley grew well. It would be unrealistic to think that everyone was able to live richly, for the poor would have to rely in the rain on a subsistence diet of barley bread, pulses and and a little meat. Vines had been in production for a long time by then, so wine and grapes would be common fare. The great problem for everyone was the weather, for a long drought or the sudden loss of fertility in the soil for any reason could be a total disaster. No wonder the Gods were called upon for continued health among the crops and people.

Clay cooking pot, with stand

A Wild Boar depicted on a coin from Lythus, Crete. c.450 B.C.

Bread

Bread in the form of barley-cakes was served with meals or eaten separately. Bread made from wheat was also eaten, and flour was sold in the markets in Athens and elsewhere. Grain from Southern Italy was shipped to Athens through the port of Piraeus and ground into a particularly soft white flour. There are some charming examples of miniature votive offerings of food to the Gods and Goddesses. Made of clay in about 300 B.C. and only a few centimetres across, they represent tiny loaves of bread and cakes arranged on a tray. Demeter, the Goddess with the care of harvest and bread, had a temple at Corinth and some of these offering trays were found in the Sanctuary. Other similar objects appear in other places, such as Boeotia so the practice was wide-spread. Later on, the Roman Army in Britain used rye as well as barley and wheat in their bread, sometimes adding cheese or spices or honey.

An Ear of Barley
– on a coin from Metapontum

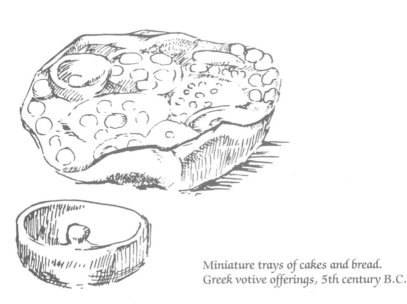

Miniature trays of cakes and bread.
Greek votive offerings, 5th century B.C.

Portable clay oven. Greek,
c.5th century B.C.

Fish

Both Greece and Rome had long coastlines and the sea provided plenty for everyone, both cheap small fish for anybody who wanted them, and expensive treats for those able to pay the price in the markets. The fish markets were well-supplied and a bell was rung at opening-time in Athens. The Romans imported fish from Sicily, and fresh mackerel was brought from the Hellespont to Rome. Smoke-houses were used to prepare the smoked fish which was available in the shops.

Cretan fishing spear or trident

The types of fish brought ashore everywhere were extraordinarily varied and both Greeks and Romans enjoyed their lightness and delicacy, often preferring fish to any kind of meat.

Flat fish such as plaice were caught in shallow waters. Odysseus' companions were said to have caught fish with hooks attached to a long pole. This was then flung out onto the ground, where the fish were collected. In later times the 'winged' flat fish such as ray and skate may still have been caught in the same way and the 'wings' were cooked with wine, vinegar, olive oil and capers, as they are today – a delicious dish if the fish are fresh from the sea.

Mullet, sea bream, flying fish, sardines, tunny and turbot, were all obtained in good quantities. They were usually baked whole and served with a covering sauce – the famous silphium sauce for choice. Crayfish, being a fresh-water species, were expensive, but quickly snapped up at the Athenian market by eager hosts hoping to give their guests something special.

Shell-fish of all kinds were in the rocky pools just for the picking. Shallow-water species, mussels, cockles, limpets, periwinkles, scallops and others were easier to obtain than conches, oysters and the larger barnacles which thrived lower down in the sea. The sea-urchins and the land urchin – the hedgehog – were both collected and cooked. These were often used as a first course at dinner – a light starter to a meal. The urchins were cooked by enclosing the prickly mass of spines or quills with mud baking, and taking off the prickly crust when cooked.

Plate decorated with fishes (torpedo fish and sea bream)
from Currae, Apulia. 4th century B.C.

Shrimp, squid and octopus were likely to be home-caught near the shore. Nowadays octopus is sometimes served with lemon juice, either hot or cold, but this is how to deal with an octopus in the old style.

First catch your octopus. It will be a small brownish shape lying in a hole under a rock – perhaps a place well-known to the locals. A bait of dead fish will be useful. Hold the tentacles and turn the stomach – a white bag – inside out, and wash well. To release the muscular tension in the tentacles, beat them as hard as you can on a stone and go on doing this until they are limp and soft. Wash. Lay the octopus on a rough rock and run it round and round with your hand. A white soapy fluff will appear. When the octopus appears pale, limp, and almost transparent (or you do) it is ready for use.

Wash well. Take the octopus, remove the ink sac and all else, retaining the tentacles. Simmer these gently for one hour. Remove, dry, cut into small pieces and leave to get cold. Pour over some olive oil and sprinkle with a little of the herb origano. If a hot dish is required, a spicy sauce can be used.

Meat

Meat, once the early days of primitive barbecues were over, was thought best when boiled or baked. Boiled meat meant putting the pieces into a cauldron over an open fire. The baked meats were cooked either over a fire or in a partly covered cooker made of hard clay, or in an enclosed oven in a casserole-type of kitchen-ware. Grills were popular and used for small items, such as sausages or chops – these grills were set low on the ground, with a fire beneath, and were made of baked clay.

Metal equipment was necessary for poking fires, hooking out meat, hanging hooks in butchers' shops and other arrangements. These were made of bronze or later, of iron. There are stone carvings which show shops in Roman Britain with meat hanging on such hooks. Knives and cleavers were in every kitchen and enough useful pots, jars, bowls, mortars and shelves, to gladden the heart of any modern cook, so there were no problems with the actual act of cooking the meats.

A favourite meat in all ages was pork. The wild pig was leaner and more tasty, but pigs were farmed and could be bought in the markets – either small, such as sucklings which were cooked whole, or cut up and made into savoury stews, or minced up even smaller with herbs and made into sausages. Sausages seem to have been the poor man's food over many centuries, although they were eaten by the elegant Romans with equal pleasure.

Cooked sausages were sold in the market-place in Athens by men

Stone relief of a shepherd and his dog. 2nd century B.C.

carrying trays of them – a spicy smell as they stood near the gate of the Agora, the market. They refreshed their stocks by using grills for the sausages before starting their trade again. Smoked pigs' knuckles were reckoned to be good, sometimes with a cheese sauce over them.

One of the greatest delicacies in Roman times was a dish unlikely to be presented at dinner today. When a pig was sent for killing at the butchers, the whole paunch was removed and was regarded as a particular luxury, suitably spiced and sauced for maximum effect. Another particular Roman delicacy was Dormouse – no now longer found on the average Mum!

Lamb and beef were eaten, although beef much less so, perhaps on religious grounds, as the sacred nature of the bull – Zeus in disguise perhaps? – made this seem less suitable except at religious festivals. Sheep were herded on the hills and green slopes and from earliest days were used for food – again, baked or stewed in a casserole, with spices and herbs. Myrtle and juniper berries were put into meat dishes, and wreaths of myrtle were worn on the heads of people at dinner. Myrtle-berries could even be put on the table for guests to chew if they wished. The picture on the next page shows the types of casseroles in which the meat stews were cooked – these are Greek, but the same kind of equipment was also used by Roman chefs. Some fat came out in the cooking, but it is likely that the wild animals carried less fat than farm-reared animals today, so olive oil was used as well. Salt was sea-salt, sold in the market and treated with more care than we do now, but an essential ingredient in the pot.

Vegetables

Vegetables were important in Greek and Roman diets to the point where the people were almost vegetarians by choice. With a climate suitable for herbs and berries, and flat plains between hills and even extensive marshes and estuaries, all sun-drenched in summer, it was a vegetarian paradise.

Myrtle and berries
Myrtus Communis

The green vegetable, *Horta,* with its delicate sharpness, is still gathered today as young and tender wild plant by cutting below ground with a knife-point and boiling the whole, to be used hot or cold. In other countries it may be called dandelion. Other plants were increasingly cultivated commercially by cuttings or seeds. Complaints about garden pests, slugs, grubs, began to make themselves heard!

Portable clay casserole cooking-pot on a brazier.
Greek. 5th century B.C.

There are accounts of asparagus plants which grew to a height of twenty feet especially in the mud of the Libyan delta. Another kind, more like the cultivated modern variety, which grew by the sea, was almost as large. Yet another variety grew in the mountains. Roman cooks used to garnish boiled lobster with asparagus.

Fennel, used for flavouring and as a vegetable, also grew in the swampy marshes of Attica, and wild celery was another water-loving edible plant. Other vegetables were picked from the abundance of wild greenstuff available, as were stinging nettles which, when picked young, make an excellent boiled dish of nutritious food. Gourds were used not so much for their food value, but for their moisture content, steeped in water and vinegar or boiled.

Cucumbers, especially from Antioch, and pumpkins, were treated in the same way. Radishes – the round ones – were also brought to market. The best lettuces came from Smyrna, although

Edible mushroom
Boletus Edulis

there were many types of this plant – it was considered not to overheat the body. Cabbage was farm-grown and popular, and onions were eaten raw with wine or cooked in different ways. Chick-peas could be eaten raw but were also boiled in water. Various bulbs were regarded as edible, and roots of the wild iris, and Jerusalem artichoke. More exotic were the palm-tops – the heads of palm trees – usually taken from the suckers springing up from the sides of the trees. Even without the New World products of potatoes and tomatoes, and other vegetables not then introduced, there was a wide variety for people to choose from.

Mushrooms were either in the fields or attached to trees – elms, oaks and beeches. They were used with care, for many were poisonous, particularly the amanita which looks very much like an edible variety. Truffles were dug up and could be bought in the markets – not as scarce or expensive as they are today.

Roman nettle
Uvtica Pilmlifera

15

Flavourings – Herbs and Spices

Thyme and sage grew on most hillsides, and marjoram was brought from the Island of Cos. Rue was best from Myra in Lycia while Cyprus provided mustard. Spike lavender was often a local product. Other flavourings were wild garlic, onions of several kinds and scallions – a kind of spring onion. Pepper was imported from the East through the trade routes in Roman times. The strong sauces so much used by Greeks and Romans were made with some or all of these – and included a particularly popular basic sauce concocted from rank fish-guts – presumably something like an elderly anchovy sauce. Yellow saffron from the meadow-land crocus was also used in sauces and as a flavouring and colouring.

The silphium plant grew wild in the dry wastes of ancient Libya, North Africa, and was at one time the main export of the city of Cyrene which showed the plant on its coinage. The

Thyme
Oridothymus Capitatus

Rue
Ruta Grareslens

Wild Parsley
Petroselinus Crispus

16

leaves and stems were crushed to produce a juice made into a sauce used chiefly for fish, but with other foods as well. It was supposed to have medicinal properties, curing asthma, epilepsy, melancholia, coughs, reptile bites and other discomforts. Its green leaves could be used as animal feed, but the strongly aromatic thick stems were also used as a vegetable for human consumption, sometimes steeped in vinegar. It seems to have grown only in that area, becoming so valuable that it was said to be worth its weight in gold. It is unlikely that we shall ever be able to try out this remarkable flavour, because it was used so greedily and exported so widely for the benefit of the city that by 300 B.C. it had become very scarce indeed and some time around 500 A.D. it became extinct. However, in its day it was one of the great glories of early cookery. It seems odd that its only disadvantage was that it proved deadly poisonous to camels.

Juniper
Uniperus Communis

Origano
Origanum Heraclesticura

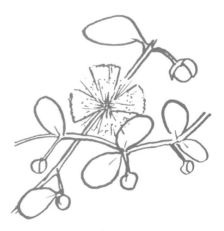

Capers
Capparis Spinosa

Fruit and Nuts

Both fresh and dried fruits were enjoyed by the Greeks and Romans. Trees of pears, mulberries, cherries and apples grew wild. There were plums, and their cousins, the damsons, so named because the first came from Damascus. Bullaces, a type of wild plum, were eaten and blackberries and other wild berries grew in profusion. Figs, both fresh and dried were sweet and so were raisins and imported Jericho dates. Pomegranates came from Cyprus, and varieties of grapes came from all over. The beautiful arbutus – the strawberry tree – had red berries which were delicious when they were ripe. Oranges were not yet seen on Roman tables, but peaches most certainly were. Sweet melons were cooling on a hot summer evening. The best quinces came from the Island of Cos.

The walnut was called the 'Royal' nut and it is still widely grown in Greece and Italy. But beech nuts were also eaten, as they still are in parts of Europe and chestnuts were used in cooking. Pine-kernels were in the markets and almonds from the Island of Naxos were particularly famous. Honey and almond cakes were good at the end of a meal. The Romans were fond of a pudding made from milk and barley-cakes which were filled with pine-kernels. Filberts were brought with dessert to table.

Olives

The olive should have a special mention. It was the main contribution to both Greek and Roman cookery. Athena, Goddess of Wisdom, Protector of Cities, was believed to have given the cultivated olive tree to Athens, whence it spread to all Greece. An olive twig can be seen on the coins of ancient Athens. The ripe black olives were beaten from the trees onto cloths spread on the ground, then collected, put into a press and crushed until the golden oil ran out – a method still used today. The oil was then stored in large pottery jars called *amphorae*. This oil was the only fuel available for the lamps of clay or metal – it gives a soft clear flame. Multiple arrangements of lights were used by the wealthy. Oil shops were common, particularly in crowded Rome, as olive trees spread all across the Aegean and Mediterranean areas. The olive berries were also eaten, used for pickling, and in many savoury dishes. When all else was used, the best wood was excellent for working and the remainder was valuable firewood.

Cultivated Olive
Olea Europaea

Honey

Of all the foods of the ancient world, honey was one of the most magical and important. Zeus, King of the Greek Gods, was believed to have been fed as a child, on goat's milk and honey and, in Roman times, the Emperor Augustus occasionally lived on a similar diet. For centuries people thought that bees were born from oxen, Zeus's animal.

The earliest way of obtaining honey was from wild bees which built their honey-combs in trees or in holes in cliffs. By the 4th century B.C. there were detailed written descriptions of bees and bee-keeping, in works by Aristotle and by other Greek and, later, Roman authors, such as Virgil, Varro, Columella.

The cleanliness and orderly ways of bees were much admired. They were well cared for. Bee diseases and parasites were understood, and there are warnings about the ravages of hornets, wasps, beetles and lizards. The Roman writer Columella thinks it better to buy swarms from a reputable source, rather than take wild swarms from the trees for their hives. Good quality bees were a cross between the Egyptian gold bee and the small black bee.

Hives were the subject of much thought. The best hives were made of reeds or cork or woven willow-twigs which left the bees cool in summer when they were most active. Hives of baked clay were used and some have survived, but they were the least successful. A round shape was preferred for all these materials, with a small entrance hole, although the clay hives had open shapes. Hives were cleaned, smoked and dried, several times a year and shelters built to protect the bees from cold winds or hot summers. At the end of the season, some honey was left for the bees for their winter food and extra feeding was advised if necessary.

In the 1st century B.C. Varro gave some ideas about providing enough nectar for the bees. He suggested sowing the seeds of nectar-producing flowers such as poppy, rose, clover, parsley, and especially of thyme, which made a particularly fine honey in Sicily. Wild flowers such as those of heathers, apple, and wild pears blossomed there, and the olive trees were said to be good for producing wax for the combs. Flowers were all-important to the flavours of the honeys used in cooking and eating, and were chosen with the same care as they are today. The Roman cook Apicius, gives a recipe for making good honey out of bad, by mixing one part of bad with two parts of good. His test for bad honey was to put a lamp-wick into the honey – if it burned, it was good.

The products of sugar cane and sugar beet now replace honey as sweeteners in most kitchens today. Formerly, the seasonal crop of honey was limited by the energy and hard work of the bees and bee-keepers, and was valued accordingly. The honey from Hymettus was, and is, particularly choice but all kinds were used in food. Sweet biscuits were often made of sesame seed and honey. Puddings had honey sauce, and honey was poured over hot pancakes, which gave off a delicious scented steam. Cheese and honey seemed to go together, either by spreading honey over the cheese or squeezing the cheese through a sieve and mixing the curd with honey or eating cheese-cakes with it. Honey-comb was also eaten in its natural form. Alongside the herbs and spices

Roman Bee-hive

in the house, there were honey-syrup and honey-vinegar. Mushrooms were often prepared with honey. As a last resort, if poisoned by eating the wrong mushrooms, honey-vinegar could be used as an antidote. Accounts of sudden death caused by careless nibbling of wild fungi seem frequent enough to need the remedy. On a lighter note, cucumber seeds were said to sprout more quickly when put into honey-syrup. Truly a wonder-food!

Lastly, honey was used as a preservative. In 323 B.C. Alexander the Great died of a fever in Babylon and his body was taken to Alexandria in Egypt for burial there. It travelled in a golden coffin which was filled with white honey.

Trade

From 2000 B.C. onwards the foods which the Greeks and Romans used came from increasingly distant places. Great fleets of commercial shipping carried the goods under recognised conditions, including the payment of duty at ports. Some of the Greek Islands were not keen to import anything which they regarded as their particular local source of revenue – wine was one of these. Much of the foodstuff was transported in barrels but grain, oil and wine were carried in large amphorae. Ships were often manned by slaves owned by the ship-masters and were oared galleys which also bore sails. Food was only one of the great array of exports and imports carried in these ships – they were traders of everything moveable, from woven cloth to papyrus for books, as long as there was a buyer waiting at the end of the voyage.

Cargoes were exchanged in early days. Once coinage had become common – it was only about 600 B.C. that the first coins appeared – then money changed hands. Coins of Greece and Rome were found far from their home mints and certain coinages, the silver owls of Athens and the silver Pegasus coins of Corinth for example, were widely used in trade. These are now found in archaeological excavations. Their regular weight and value made them acceptable over great distances.

All this brings a picture of a busy, progressive, market-system. The markets themselves, either on the quaysides or in the cities, were at times overflowing with produce and temptations. The fish stalls, butchers' shops, vegetable and fruit displays, pastrycooks' and bakers' trays, cheese and wine shops were all to be seen Athens and Rome. Fish-pedlars and sausage-men wandered among the crowds. But traders move about, and the smaller market-towns were ready to oblige customers with local produce as well as some of the other exotics brought in to them.

So much for food – now there should be something liquid to ease the dry dust of these warm climates . . .

Silphium was at one time the major export of the city of Cyrene, and is here depicted on one of its coins. It became so valuable that it was said to be worth its weight in gold.

DRINK

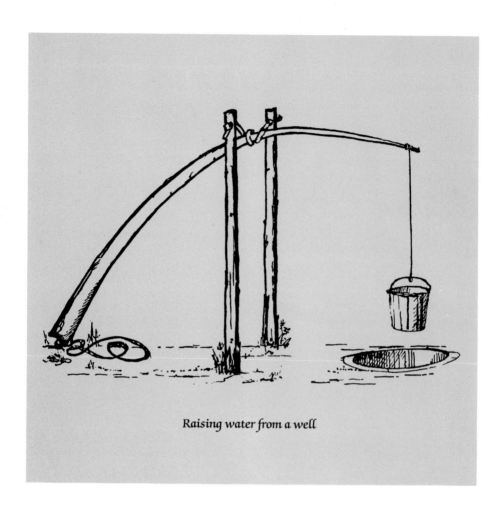

Raising water from a well

WINE AND WATER were the drinks of the old world, and the palates of ancient days were as delicate with one as with the other. In both cases, time and trouble were taken, sometimes bringing wine and water by ship or cart from far distances but also using the rich produce of spring and vine near home. There was no tea, no coffee, chocolate or even lemonade, lemons being later arrivals in Greece and Italy.

Water

Some people simply drank water, either by choice or because the effects of wine, including unmixed wine, were sometimes believed to reduce a person's creative ability. Water used for wine-mixing was carefully chosen and brought to the house when required. The Greeks used a large jar called a hydria for carrying water.

Spring water, fresh from the

24

mountains or from clean earth, was greatly valued and was occasionally scented with flowers or herbs. Many of these springs became famous for their purity and coolness, as at Tilphossa in Boeotia. The Castalian spring at Delphi still runs from a cleft in the mountain rocks of Parnassus and down through the valley below. This spring was one of many which were revered because of their proximity to temples – in this case, that of Apollo.

The pleasant flavour of the springs in Paphlagonia was thought to be like wine, and there were other notable flavours to be found elsewhere. Boiled water was used when any supply was suspected of being spoilt by impurities. There were springs of warm water in some places, which would not be surprising in an area so prone to earthquakes. Larissa was one of these. Other water tasted salty, bitter or oily and some was taken medicinally from well-known sources where mineral salts were present. The Roman Army in Britain were able to go to Bath for a cure and 'taking the waters' at that Spa is still popular today.

The Romans, brilliant and practical engineers, decided to bring water into the towns. Their aqueducts carried fresh potable water from the hills above Rome down to the City where the population was growing continually over the centuries. Aqueducts were built in Gaul (France) at Avignon and other parts of the Empire received the benefit of these advanced and amazing constructions. Equally practical, the Roman engineers provided a sewerage system to carry away City effluent.

Wine

Wine was the necessity and the pride of Greece for much further back in time than in recorded history. Dionysus, the legendary God of wine, had his first home in Thrace – north of Greece – where the ceremonies connected with his worship celebrated the use of wine. A thousand years B.C. saw the cult of Dionysus flourishing and moving south to Greece and the Peloponnese. Here the worship became extremely popular with orgiastic sessions of drinking and dancing, which sometimes ended with the tearing apart and eating of live animals. This was supposed to give the eater all the virtues of the animal – if it represented the God, so much the better. Women, particularly, took part in this ritual excitement with a good deal of enthusiasm, probably also chewing leaves of ivy or of other plants with narcotic properties. Dionysus had another name – Bacchus, and in this name he was the God of vegetation and green growth, particularly of vines. The Dionysus/Bacchus God held the old classical world in his hand at every meal.

Production

There seems good reason to believe that the grape vines and wines of Greece and Rome were first produced and developed in Thrace. This was always a famous wine-making area. At one time the vines were allowed to twine their way up into trees where the grapes hung in festoons until collected by harvesters with ladders. This produced plenty of pleasant drink, but the sweetest wines came from the low-growing pruned vines which ripened the fruit in sheltered sunshine near the soil. Both high and low growing vines

*The wine god Dionysius holding a Kantharos (drinking cup)
and a vine-branch, the symbols of his divinity*

were later grown in Greece and Italy. In Campania, in Italy, the harvesters were able to have funeral expenses included in contracts because of the danger of falling from the high-growing vines, but this privilege had died out by 300 B.C.

The varieties of grapes ripened and were harvested at different seasons. Hardier types were developed away from the central warm area which could also be planted higher up the mountain slopes. The wine of kings, the legendary drink of Nestor and Odysseus, was made from the juice which dripped from the piles of grapes left lying in the sun before work started on them – a taste long gone. The grapes were then gathered and trodden in large vats, and the best juice was put to ferment. The second-quality wine which was made by crushing all the remainder – the must – was later used separately. The fermentation vats were left for six months, constantly being skimmed to take away any bits or seeds and twigs which came to the surface. The wine was then poured into large amphorae to be matured and stored until ready for use. The Greeks had a great advantage over other people when they discovered how to produce non-porous hard pottery which meant that impurities were kept out of the wine. This had always been a problem in the past. When sealed with clay and pitch, the wine could be left for years without deterioration. Indeed, there were wines of full flavour said to be a hundred years old. The only drawback was that the Greeks did not know how to stop fermentation, so that the wines were often quite strong – one guess was put at about 17% alcohol – but unlikely to have been stronger. As

Grape Vine on a coin from Maronea

honey was the only sweetener of the day, the sweet wines were particularly welcomed.

The Roman commercial vineyards really began when Greek immigrants started to settle in Southern Italy, in Campania and in Sicily. This was before 300 B.C. and proof that the vine – and the wine – did indeed travel. In the next hundred years planting, pruning, gathering and fermenting established. Romans, Egyptians and others, still found Greek wine the best and it was their first choice, but the older vintages of Greece began to decline and suitable soils were available on the volcanic slopes of the mountains of Italy. By 150 A.D. the great Greek wines were only legends and so the output from Campania increased. These wines were exported and took over the trade almost completely, although a few Greek Islands continued to produce small amounts.

Varieties

Some of the finest of the old Greek vintages came from the Island of Lesbos. The Islands and coasts, with their spare volcanic soils and open sunlit spaces had long-established vineyards which continued well into Roman times. Lesbian wine was valued for the length of time in which its bouquet was held in the amphorae. As the export market for it was almost infinite and duty had to be paid on arrival in other ports, it was expensive. Some of it was shipped in bulk on long journeys, but it 'travelled well'.

The Thracian coast and areas surrounding it were also providers of famous quality and quantity. They were said to have had a wonderful smell of ripe apples – a luxurious aroma in those times when sweetness was rare. A modern traveller, H. Warren Allen, recently visited the Island of Thasos. He tasted the local wine and to his delight found that the warm scent of apples still lay on its breath. After 2,500 years, as he says, still true to type. No doubt there is more where that came from?

Another famous wine of ancient Greece was called *Saprias* – a 'mellow' flavour. It may have been made in several areas. In 500 B.C. it was regarded as a great treat and much sought after. It was said that, even after many years of storage, when the seals and stopper were removed from the amphora, the room was filled with the scent of flowers.

The Roman wines of quality were the *Falernian*, from central Italy and the produce of Campania and Sicily. Falernian was said to be at its best after ten years, and good after fifteen or twenty. The soil of this area was right – not too rich and with the dry warmth of the sun reflected by its

Odysseus, blown across the sea on a raft of amphoras by Boreas, the North Wind

volcanic nature. Training and setting the plants had been introduced long ago and by the time – say 100 A.D. – when the Greek vineyards were diminishing, the Campanian ones were well established.

Using Wine

Mulled wine was enjoyed in the winter. This was not heated in a pot, but wine was poured carefully into hot water in whatever proportions were wanted.

In the summer, wine had snow added to it for a drink which was a unique pleasure in a Mediterranean heat-wave. The mountains which were white-capped all winter and most of the summer provided the snow and ice. This was collected during the winter and stored underground in pits lined and covered with straw and branches of oak. The ice-houses of later Europe served the same purpose. The snow would have the effect of diluting the wine, or it could be chilled with ice. Alexander the Great took his Army through some of the hot stony valleys of the Egyptian desert and even here pits were dug and ice and snow brought in and preserved deep under the surface, ready for use later on.

In Roman times some of the Islands made a very strange product indeed. The wines of Rhodes and Cos of that period were very cheap poor quality, and to make them more colourful and to enhance their taste, salt or sea-water was added. This was considered suitable for slaves and poor people. We even have a recipe.

Rhodian Wine Jar
2nd century B.C.

10	parts new wine
2	parts vinegar
2	parts boiled-down must
50	parts fresh water
1½	parts sea water

A Greek wine cup or Skyphos decorated with an owl

The pitch used in sealing the amphorae was not the origin of the resinous flavour of the present-day wine called Retsina as is sometimes thought. The use of pine-cone resin was known in both Greece and Italy from about 300 B.C. It was put into wine in the form of a powder and was believed to have antiseptic properties. This was used in areas where the vine grew lush and leafy and in quantity – not the best soil for quality production. Olympia, on the Peloponnese, was such a place. The powdered resin was put into a bag and then into the vats for twenty days. It was known as 'headache wine' for obvious reasons. Also it was very cheap, as Retsina still is today.

Sophisticated Greeks and Romans hardly ever drank unmixed wine and looked down on a man who was greedy for wine. Wine was mixed with pure water from springs or fountains or from deep wells in towns, as in Athens, where they can still be seen. Sometimes the mixture was half and half, sometimes less wine. In early days the water was added to the wine, but later the wine was floated onto the water, in exact proportions as required by the host. The taste of the wine mattered a great deal, and the cost of the best vintages made this mixing an extra convenience.

Commerce

Trading in wine went on through Greek and Roman times. Archaeologists are discovering the great extent of the trade as they find areas at the bottom of the seas littered with sunken merchant vessels, some loaded with amphorae still in place. For ordinary short-distance movement, large goat-skins were used.

30

A baby-feeder from Apulia in the form of a mule
with wine panniers – the tail forms the spout

Silver Hellenistic Roman Wine Jug

For bigger cargoes by sea, wine was shipped in amphorae – early Greek ones held about 38.5 litres and later ones 29.5 litres. For bulk trading really enormous vats – like huge amphorae – were used. Because the seals were so cleverly made, using pitch and clay, some of the pots are still sealed, even showing the sign of the vineyard from which they came. Some amphorae have on them the design of the City or State of origin and those designs are also on their coins. Trading activities spread to most Aegean and Mediterranean countries, to Egypt and, if necessary, to the Roman armies in their stations abroad.

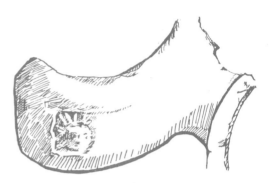

Handle of an Amphora, showing Helios, the badge of the ancient city of Rhodes

The amphorae in which the wine was delivered – such fine useful pottery – were an improvement on those of most people who bought the contents. To prevent breakages, boards with holes in them were built into the ships so that the jars could stand upright. Otherwise they were stacked horizontally in layers. Sometimes sand was used to steady the amphorae, both on the ships and afterwards in the shops or in private cellars. As to numbers – these boats might be 120 ft. long and carried two or three thousand amphorae – a vast cargo and one repeated constantly in order to keep up an adequate supply for the customers. The wine from Campania came in a steady and lucrative stream for centuries.

Delivery to the Roman Army in Britain was typical of the pattern of wine sales. The arrangements for shipping came through commercial traders, of whom there were many. These often had connections in Gaul – France. Marseilles had been a Greek colony and, as well as being a useful port in transit, it was able to supply wine from the region. The Romans also drank wine from Marseilles and considered it good. German suppliers traded cargoes from Italy through France to Britain. The Sixth Legion at York had wine delivered to them officially, but shops were also opened in places available to the soldiery – such as near Hadrian's Wall. Here small amounts of good wine could be consumed for pleasure, rather than the strange local brew of mead. To protect the Italian wine trade, no part of Britain under Roman rule was allowed to grow vines, and this law was not changed until 281 A.D. In fact, the climate was rarely suitable for the quantity of wine-producing vines which needed to be grown, although grapes were cultivated and the tools for doing so have been found in Hertfordshire.

Wine Cups

Early drinking cups were made of clay or metal. The Greek talent for making fine painted pottery was taken, over the centuries, to brilliant heights. The vessels were light, shaped on a wheel, and painted by artists whose work was later collected by Roman admirers. Metal cups, jugs and bowls were made of gold, silver, bronze, even pewter had a fashionable period. The gold cups from Mycenae, now over 3,000 years old are marvellous works of art. Silver was used in Roman times in great quantities and is still being found on Roman sites in Britain and elsewhere. Glass was a late arrival on the scene. It came first from Egypt, imported while wine was being exported from Greece. By 300 B.C. glass vessels were part of table ware in rich households. Later, Romans made their own glass in their own workshops. Ancient glass was not as clear as modern glass, but it was often coloured with patterns and stripes. The Army in Britain received its glass and bronze through the German traders and this came from several places, including France, Italy and Germany itself where there was a glass industry. As the Roman Army had left Britain by 400 A.D. these traders must have been making their profits before then.

Good Drinking

All in all, wine-drinking had a very serious and special place in people's daily lives. Roman society used the Greek mode of drinking wine mixed with water, first making sure that a libation to the Gods was made in undiluted wine. This was offered by pouring out a small quantity onto the ground, no doubt with a suitable prayer. The mixing of wine was done so that men and women could drink enough to relax and make them talk and chatter, but not enough to make them stupid. The good host would not ask a guest to dinner and then trouble him by making him uncomfortable or look foolish. Mixed wine would quench the thirst in a hot climate and release the taste and scents of the various wines to give pleasure with no after-effects. Sometimes a little unmixed wine was served at the end of a meal, but the idea of anyone but the Gods receiving it before a meal was very unusual and frowned upon. It was only in the late days of the Roman Empire, when the old dignities of societies were passing, that the messy banquets of legend were held. Early Greeks would have looked with disdain on such vulgarity and ostentation – at least the early author Athenaeus, who lived in Greece, would have us believe so!

BE MERRY

HAVING A GOOD TIME in Ancient Greece meant, for choice, the delights of conversation. People talked with unlimited endurance. They planned evenings with friends and invited others who were known to be amusing, interesting, or just good company. The circles of coffee-drinkers outside the modern tavernas are pale descendants of such excitements of the past. In many of the old Greek legends there are accounts of gatherings of friends which must have been familiar to the story-tellers, who may themselves have been sitting among such a group. Stories of travellers were told and the talk, welcoming drink and food, are described in detail. As early

Greece was made up of many small States, with their own governments and manners, returning travellers would be full of new tales and ideas. In later, more sophisticated days – say 500 B.C. the intellectuals used a conversation like this for thoughtful and erudite discussion, called a *symposium*, but the basic pattern remained the same. Roman life usually followed the Greek style although, as the centuries passed, Roman parties began to have more emphasis on the food and drink. However, the bright, artistic, and fashionable members of high society still enjoyed pitting their wits against each other with conversational artillery.

A Youth carrying a couch and three-legged table in preparation for a symposium

Kantharos or wine cup

36

A Greek Party

A typical Greek party of about 350 B.C. would start with the host inviting a congenial group of friends, both men and women. They were offered mixed wine, as expensive as the host thought suitable for the occasion, either wine from Lesbos if he wished to impress the company or wine from Thrace or elsewhere for a less important group. The guests ate with knives, spoons and fingers, sitting on chairs or reclining on couches, leaning on one elbow. The meal would be good, beginning with a small serving of raw dried fish, a sea-urchin or a little pickled turnip.

There would then be the main dish of vegetables dressed with oil, and some meat or fish with sauce, followed by fruit or honey-cakes or other sweet dessert. Sometimes meals were taken without meat, but usually with barley bread and pulses. The chatter and gossip and the laughing jokes and counter-jokes went on after the meal, while the wine-cups were refilled by cup-bearers. Cup-bearers were boys or girls who were trained to take wine from the amphorae, mix it in the bowls, and serve it from the jugs which they carried. After a while, the guests would turn to playing the game of *Kottabos* which continued until everyone was tired and went home.

Kottabos seems to have been the 'Monopoly' of ancient Greece. It put a sort of spell over the players and became almost an obsession with them. Not only was it competitive and exciting, but required skill and practice to the point where tutors were employed to teach the finer points, especially to young people. Sometimes a separate room was set aside for the game. Both men and women played and it was popular for centuries.

*An Etruscan
Kottabos Manos*

A symposium attended by six men reclining and feasting beneath Vines (the figure in the centre is a Gorgon's head, probably intended to ward-off evil spirits)

The players of Kottabos had to leave the last few drops of of wine in the cup and, bending the arm back and over, throw the dregs accurately at a small target, the plastinx. There are vases with pictures of people doing this. The target was on top of the Kottabos stand which itself stood on a narrow column at the end of a room. There was a small tray on the Kottabos stand and when the target was hit, the tray fell down with a clatter, to the sound of cheers and laughter. A little bronze figure, called a *Manus,* was also on the stand and presented an extra hazard to the players. The clattering sound of the falling tray was sometimes used for fortune-telling, according to the way it fell or bounced. In one version a basin of water was placed below the stand and small dishes were floated in it, so increasing the variety of possible sounds. Bets were placed on results of contests. Presentation cups were given for winners of properly organized competitions and, although some of the prizes were for fun – a kiss – some were of valuable silver dishes. In any case, a real game for a party!

A Party for Persians

Not all feasts went exactly as planned. When, in the 5th century B.C., the Army of the Persians under the Great King, Xerxes, approached mainland cities belonging to the Island of Thasos, the Thasians tried to soften up the soldiers by providing a huge banquet. More silver cups and mixing-bowls had to be specially made for such a number and a generous citizen put up the money to make a show. The army arrived and ate and drank. When they left, however, they took the silverware with them, leaving the sponsor with a severe problem. Xerxes himself was in the habit of honouring his own birthday with a banquet for 15,000 men of his Army, in true Persian luxury, spending the equivalent of 160 Roman denarii (silver coins) per man. Xerxes was probably not the man you would invite for a drink a second time, unless you wished to face ruin. The Spartans, on the other hand, were reputed to serve food so terrible that no-one in his right mind would eat it.

A Roman Party

A typical social evening given by a wealthy Roman citizen in about 150 A.D. would be different from the earlier Greek one already described. The furnishings of the couches for the guests and the decorations in the hall had a general appearance of greater luxury. After dark, a variety of oil-lamps would be lit, hanging or on stands, some with several lights, like chandeliers. Dinner started in the late afternoon and the guests would be

A slave-girl, walking carefully so as not to spill the wine from the cup she is carrying

A terracotta Roman lamp
with the Christian monogram

The meal would begin with a light dish of eggs, or perhaps a plate of oysters. Oysters were kept in fish-ponds for sale to the wealthy Romans and would not be cheap enough for poor people to eat. The main course would consist of several dishes, the most important being an animal roasted and served whole, such as a small pig or lamb. The roasted animals were cooked in a hot oven while a slave turned it slowly and basted the meat with spicy sauce or honey. The sauce would also be offered with the meat. Once again, fingers and knives were used, table-forks being a comparatively modern invention.

Other dishes would be presented before or with the most important one, pork or veal, or a roast peacock or two, even something exotic such as a flamingo, or even a platter of flamingo tongues. Lampreys were rich people's food served at feasts, and were also kept in fish-pools for commercial sale. Lampreys are eel-like sea-creatures which fix themselves to rocks with suckers and were popular food in Mediaeval as well as Roman times.

There was a good deal of one-up-manship and showing off at these feasts – rare foodstuffs being obtained from foreign countries or from parts of the expanding Empire, especially the spices and peppers from the East which accompanied everything. Vegetables were plentiful and greatly enjoyed, and there were beans, grains of many kinds, dresssed with sauce or olive oil. Mixed wine was served during the whole meal.

The final course was a sweet one. There was a variety of fruits brought in on decorated platters – pomegranates, apples, pears, peaches, dates, figs, grapes and many more. Honey-cakes

attended by numbers of house-slaves, some of whom played music during the evening.

Guests began and finished each meal with clear water poured over their hands. Greeks and Romans were particular about cleanliness before eating, and hand-basins and towels were brought by slaves. Sometimes the water was warmed and scented. At the end of the meal, slaves cleared away the dirty dishes, removed the tables, and brought fresh water in the hand-basins. After drying their hands, the guests were free to replace their flowered wreaths on their heads, before continuing to enjoy the entertainment.

were popular, also a Roman version of ice-cream, using the snow and ice as they did for wine. Boiled-down sweet grape juice produced a sugary sauce. With the dessert there were other wines and later on the tables were removed. The entertainers provided by the host came to give their performances while the guests on their couches spent a convivial evening. It was rather a formal evening on these occasions but there were also the groups of friends who met in their own homes for traditional conversations. By the 4th century in Rome, learned guests would have been able to find subjects for argument in many private and public libraries in the City. At that time there were over 25 public libraries there, which contained books in the form of papyrus rolls.

Quince

Figs (Ficus Carica) and a strawberry tree (Arbutus Unedo)

41

A Party in Britain

The Roman Army in Britain was at the outer coldest edge of the Roman Empire, but even here the soldiers had their home comforts. Not only was wine imported for them – a drink almost unknown to the local population – but olive oil as well. Olive oil was part of the staple diet in Rome and no doubt the troops were happy to eat familiar food. The oil came from Spain, along the same sea-routes as the wine from France. The soldiers would have been overjoyed at the quantity of fine oysters available on every shore. The first indication of a Roman site for an archaeologist is often a pile of ancient oyster-shells. Certainly the Romans looked after their men and gave them a chance to do as well as the Army left in comfort in Rome. Even chariot-racing, baths and theatres were provided – not only in this northern outpost but in other extensions of the Empire.

Wreaths

The wreaths worn on their heads by dinner guests were not matters to be taken lightly. The leaves and flowers were carefully selected for their effect and wreaths could be bought from a wreath-maker after due consideration. For parties, the brightest and most perfumed flowers were used in their proper season – the host of the feast being particularly well decorated. Wild flowers, so abundant still in these areas, were gathered and twisted into head-wreaths or into longer strands to wear around the neck. Violets, narcissus, lilies, chrysanthemums, day-lilies, rose-campion, irises, wall-flowers, melilot, poppies, soap-wort, thyme and everything else beautiful or scented was brought into use. The art of taking stem cuttings from plants such as roses or root cuttings from irises and thyme and similar plants, and the knowledge of how to force

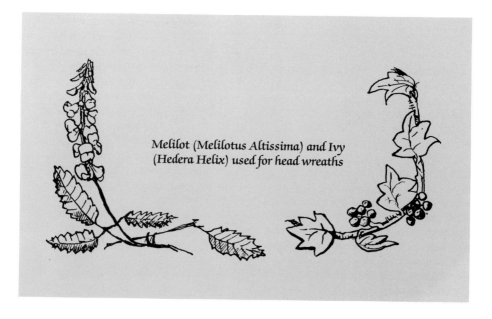

Melilot (Melilotus Altissima) and Ivy
(Hedera Helix) used for head wreaths

Laurel
Laureno Nobilis

new growth by potting up slips of plants, were all well established in Greek and Roman times. The wreath-makers used the results. Some wreaths were named after the areas in which they grew, or for other reasons. Circlets of the pink lotus which grew around Alexandria in Egypt were called *Antinoeios* because, when the Roman Emperor Hadrian killed a great lion in Libya near Alexandria while on a hunting trip, the Alexandrians told him that the pink flower was very rare and they called the wreath after Hadrian's favourite, Antinous. There was also a blue form of the lotus, said to be more common.

Other wreaths had properties beyond their function of decoration. Binding the head with a twist of myrtle was supposed to dispel the fumes of wine. Roses had a sedative power and a cooling effect as well as a pleasant scent. Laurel was recommended if attending a drinking bout but marjoram was thought to stupefy and oppress the head – this last was said to grow well in Egypt. Gillyflowers, however, would excite the nerves in the head. The rites of Dionysus were celebrated with the people twining ivy-leaves into their wreaths – this not only looked very nice, with little bunches of

berries among the green, but warded off headaches. Wreaths of 'gold' flowers were used as offerings to the Gods – just a simple gesture, probably using the brilliant yellow wild chrysanthemums which still flourish. Wreaths of these 'gold' flowers hanging on doors or even in cars are frequent decorations today during the Easter festivals in Greece – they are strung through the centres, like beads. Wreaths of real gold leaves and flowers have been found from Mycenean times onwards and they are fine and beautifully made, usually as memorials to the dead or for special ceremonial occasions.

Dancing

Dancing was supposed by the Greeks to be an invention of ancient Greece but, in view of its wide appeal, that sounds like boasting. It is true that dancing in Greece had an importance which made it part of everyone's lives. There were none of the casual dances organized for people to attend but there were set occasions at which people danced or watched others.

The dances which took place at religious festivals were part of the celebrations offered to the Gods. Sometimes processions of dancers went to the temples and the public joined in. It was common for sacrifices of animals to be made on religious occasions and the meat was cooked and shared among the onlookers. They drank wine, possibly ate barley cakes, sang and danced, and a good time was had by all. The God Dionysus had a particularly riotous following, with the 'mountain-dance' winding its torchlit path noisily up through the trees. Goddesses also had similar types of worship, with the same mixture of

A comic actor and acrobat

A cock fight c.550–525 B.C.

serious offerings and enjoyable dances. Greek soldiers in full armour joined in pyrrhic dances before battle – this used steps which represented the fighting which was soon to start. An intricate dance with complicated movements was performed at Knossus, on the Island of Crete. This was in memory of the day when Athenian youths and maidens were no longer taken into the Minotaur's winding maze of the Labyrinth and Athens was free from King Minos.

Dancing had other definite places on the special days which occurred in family or country life. Weddings, Funerals, Birthdays and rejoicing of all kinds were a time for dancing since it was an important part of the festivity, often accompanied by wine, singing, or music. There were men's dances and women's dances and these were distinctly different in various parts of Greece, quite recognizable by the people of their day.

Amusements

Entertainment by paid performers was common and tumblers and jugglers were very popular in all centuries. A favourite juggler with both Greeks and Romans – presumably a travelling man – was Matreas from Alexandria in Egypt who seems to have been an outspoken wit as well, who poked fun at serious philosophers. In Athens there was a marionette-player called Potheinus, and many jugglers. Conjurers with 'magical tricks' were great stuff and one, Cratinthenes, was able to make fire appear 'spontaneously'. There were clowns, one particularly noted for imitating boxers and wrestlers. There were dancing-girls, harp-girls and flute-girls. Famous courtesans expected to

Boy with a hoop, carrying a plate of food covered with a napkin

be paid well for their work and some became popular because of their conversation and comments which could be quoted with glee around the market places. Long ago, the Celts were said to have paid fighting men to entertain them in their own homes with mock fights, which sometimes went too far and ended in death – naturally a shockingly barbaric idea to elegant Greeks and Romans.

The Roman Gods were similar to the Greek Gods but with different names and often with different worship and ceremonies. Dancing was not usually done for religious reasons. However, skilled slaves were employed to dance and sing in private homes, perhaps in animal masks or fancy costumes. Dinner parties sometimes ended with general hilarity and dancing. The later Roman Emperors gave great public entertainments which at one time were shows of fighting gladiators and animals in the arena. Public shows and displays of dancing became

The Priestess of Dionysius and her attendants dispensing wine

increasingly popular, paid for by the Emperors and put on by professional actors. These turned into low comedy to amuse the citizens and keep them cheerful, but the shows became increasingly vulgar and obscene, and got worse. Not until the influence of Christianity was strong enough did these performances come to an end.

More acceptable as entertainment were the chariot races where money was laid out in bets as the charioteers swung the horses round the arenas.

Ordinary people went to these for a day out – to cheer on their favourites and buy a sausage to eat as they watched. Rich men owned these chariots, men and horses, and then went to see them win. Afterwards, the baths were there for rest and talk about the day's excitement – the equivalent of the modern club-house, but with steam. And there was always the theatre for the bored and gloomy, showing some of the best comic plays ever written.

46

A Special Time

In Italy, in the Province of Latium, of which Rome was the capital city, the Festival of Saturnalia was held. Saturnus was the legendary figure who was believed to have invented agriculture and so the end of the harvest season, December, was a time of rest and release from labour. During this period, all law courts, schools, commerce, civil services, farming and other work ceased completely. Both rich and poor expected to enjoy themselves and give up ordinary daily tasks. Slaves, in particular, had their great day. Not only did they stop work, but they changed places with their owners, even exchanging clothes with them and mixing freely as citizens (which they were not) in the town. The masters provided their slaves with banquets and entertainment, serving them as richly as they had been served themselves. For once, slaves had complete freedom of speech. In Rome, children served the slaves at table while the masters did the domestic duties. It was a kind of carnival, with most people wearing different clothes – either fancy-dress or, more likely, the little felt or woollen cap, the *pileus*, usually only worn by citizens. Everyone, slave or master, was on equal terms, and the streets were filled with shouting and noisy crowds, some calling 'Io Saturnalia' and some carrying tapers. Unusually, gambling was permitted on this sacred day. In private homes where parties were going on, it was amusing to elect an imitation 'King' and enjoy a mock ceremony around his 'court'. This was the chief public and universal time for all in Rome, when normal habits were dismissed and turned upside-down. Of course, there were the usual reasons given, but for the slaves most of all, these were the days to remember.

Two boys filling wine cups from a 'column-crater' in which wine would have been mixed with water

47

Further Reading

Allen H.W. *History of Wine.*

American School of Classical Studies at Athens – many excellent picture books.

Athenaeus. (Trans.) Lock Classical Library

Bailey D.M. *Greek and Roman Pottery Lamps.* British Museum. 1963

Bisley A. *Life in Roman Britain.* Batsford Putnam. 1964

Crane E. *The Archaeology of Beekeeping.* Duckworth. 1983

Edwards J. (Trans.) *Roman Cookery of Apicius.* Hartley & Monks Ltd. 1984

Fraser H.M. *Beekeeping in Antiquity.* U.L.P. 1951

Muir's Atlas of Ancient Classical History. 1982

Niebuhr A.D. *Herbs of Greece.* N.E. Unit of Herb Society of America. 1970

Oxford Classical Dictionary. O.U.P. 2nd Ed. 1969

Royal Horticultural Society. *Flowers of Greece.* Wisley Handbook 9. 1972

Seltman C. *Greek Coins.* Methuen. 1955

Seltman C. *Wine in the Ancient World.*

Smith W. *Dictionary of Greek and Roman Antiquities.* 1842

Stabb J.M. *Home Book of Greek Cookery.* Faber. 1963

Vickers M. *Greek Vases.* Ashmolean Museum. 1982